OLUSOLA OSINOIKI

UNDERSTANDING THE LORD'S PRAYER

Understanding the Lord's Prayer

ISBN 978-1-7375905-9-0
Second Edition 2023
Published by Josh Publications
Email: solaosinoiki@googlemail.com

All Scriptures are taken from the King James Version of the Bible.

Cover and Page Designs by Dewalette Creations
dewalette@gmail.com

Contents

ACKNOWLEDGEMENTS

I would like to start by thanking the Author of Life, God the creator of all things—He who gives us all things to enjoy.

I would also like to thank my darling wife Kunbi, for her support and editing work on this project.

Thanks also to my son Olumide (Olu) for allowing daddy the time to work on this project. We can now read your comics together and big welcome to Olamide (Ola).

I acknowledge the support and friendship of the foundational members of Josh Publications birthed in Obafemi Awolowo University Ife, Nigeria; Tayo Smith (Nee Onifade), Funke Ojo, Lola (Nee Abida- kun), Kolade Ojo-Osagie. Thanks for your support and inspiration. Thanks to all in Runnymede Chris-tian Fellowship, Egham who stood shoulder-to-shoulder with me.

Many thanks to Julia Food, Kevin and Rosie Lewis, Kola Tayo and Pastor Taiwo Jayieoba for the time spent proofreading the manuscript of this book. My thanks also to Pastor Dave Wells of Harvest City Church Regina Canada for writing the foreword.

My thanks also to Tokunbo Emmanuel, my publisher, for all his help and encouragement.

Finally, my thanks to everyone, for taking the time to read this book. May the entrance of God's word bring light to your path.

Olusola Osinoiki
Josh Publications

Acknowledgements for Second Edition

As we planned to republish this book, I realized that many years had passed since the first print, and I wanted to write a new acknowledgement. Thankfully, my publisher indulged me, so here we go.

First and foremost, I want to express my gratitude to God for giving me the opportunity to author this book. Additionally, I want to thank Jesus for bestowing upon us such a powerful prayer, which has been passed down from his disciples to the church.

I would also like to acknowledge the unwavering support of my lovely wife, Morounkunbi, as well as the encouragement of my four wonderful children: Olu, Funso, Ola, and Lola. They have been incredible cheerleaders, always motivating me to follow God's lead in every aspect of my life - whether it be a trip, a book, a speaking engagement, or even just taking some time for rest. Family is one of the most powerful units we can have, and I am truly blessed with a great one.

The reason for writing a new acknowledgement is to highlight that we are currently living in a world that is confused about the role of God, the church, and even prayer. Therefore, I want to express my appreciation to everyone who recognizes the power of prayer, whether it is in their family, church, school, community, or workplace. Jesus taught us how to pray with his powerful prayer, which is not a formula but rather a pattern of prayer.

Finally, I want to acknowledge you for taking the time to read this. Even in a world dominated by ChatGPT and technology, it is crucial that we remain still and listen to the heart of God when it comes to prayer.

Sola Osinoiki

To all praying men and women

FOREWORD

Many Christians struggle in the area of prayer. They often feel condemned for their lack of prayer and don't have the confidence to believe their prayers are being heard. Oftentimes, when we come to God in prayer we come with our "wish list" and then hurry out of God's presence. This leaves us with a feeling of dissatisfaction as we know deep inside that there must be a "better way" to relate to God than this. Olusola gives us that "better way". He has done an excellent job of taking the Lord's prayer and giving us a pattern for prayer that we can follow with confidence. He shares with us the proper way and attitude in which to approach God. By praying according to the Lord's prayer we have the satisfaction that we are approaching God in the manner in which He wants to be approached and we can leave God's presence with the assurance that we are "relating to God as our Father and not just "using Him". We have the sure knowledge that we are praying Biblical prayers that are effective.

I trust that you will be as enlightened as I was in reading this book and that you will be inspired to pray.

David Wells
Senior Pastor, Harvest City Church
Regina, Saskatchewan, Canada

Introduction

Prayer is a powerful and mysterious spiritual activity that brings wonder and blessings.

The power of prayer lies not in how much we pray, but in how much our prayers align with the principles of prayer. Prayer is not to be omitted, it is not to be rushed and it is not to be muddled. We are to approach God in prayer, not only soberly but also with a sound mind.

Prayer is an important ingredient for spiritual growth and your fellowship with the Lord; it makes you strong in the Lord. Prayer builds you up in the Lord.

> *"But ye, beloved, building up yourselves on your most holy faith, praying in the Holy Ghost."* **Jude 20**

The Bible says in Luke 18:1, "*Men ought always to pray, and not to faint.*" What an encouragement and a challenge for us all to keep an attitude of prayer and to keep praying because this is what we ought to do.

Prayer is a two-way communication link between God and us. In prayer, we pour out our hearts to the Lord in faith, making intercession, supplications, giving thanks and praise to Him. In prayer, we also have the privilege of having the Lord speak to us, either through an inner witness or directly. The Lord loves to listen to the voices of His children. The Psalmist confirms this in Psalms 65:2: "*O thou that hearest prayer unto thee shall all flesh come*". God loves to speak to us His children; He delights in us and therefore loves to speak words of encouragement to us as well as words of correction.

Prayer is so simple and yet it could be very difficult. It becomes difficult and probably boring when we do not know how to pray. It can easily become monotonous if we do not allow the Lord to lead us in prayer. Prayer becomes easy, enjoyable and a delight once we know how to pray. The Bible says God's people are destroyed for lack of knowledge (Hosea 4:6). Even Jesus' disciples who were with Him during His ministry did not know how to pray, as evidenced by their request:

> *"And it came to pass, that, as he was praying in a certain place, when he ceased, one of his disciples said unto him, Lord, teach us to pray, as John also taught his disciples."* **Luke 11:1**

We find out, as we read on, that the Lord gave them what we today call, "The Lord's Prayer".

In Matthew 6:9, Jesus said to His disciples: "*After this manner therefore pray ye: Our Father which art in heaven. Hallowed be thy name.*" He was not only giving them a prayer for that moment, but He was also giving them the key principles or elements of prayer. The Lord would not have intended that they take the prayer as a mere recital. In fact, Jesus never again repeats the prayer in the course of His ministry, but the pattern of the prayer is repeated all through scripture. Today, many people recite the Lord's Prayer or pray it without a clear understanding of what it means. Hence, it does not produce faith and joy; rather it is dry and meaningless. The format of the Lord's Prayer is so extensive that if you pray according to the format from the heart, you would have covered every aspect of prayer.

Over the years, many of us have prayed the Lord's Prayer without realizing the depth of its meaning. We have spent time in prayer almost as though wandering through a maze. We seek to understand prayer, but the more we try the less we understand, mainly because we are trying in our strength and from our understanding of what prayer is or think it. There is a way to approach the throne of grace. Jesus knows the way, and in fact, He is the way. Jesus is the only way to the Father, therefore He could teach His disciples the principles of prayer, based on His own true experience of prayer. Jesus demonstrates through the prayer He prayed with the disciples, the elements and principles of true prayer. In Luke 11, He did not just recite a prayer to them. He prayed it and showed us by example what prayer is.

The Lord's Prayer has been neglected and misused in our present day. It has also been criticized greatly. In reality, the prayer in both its principles and the actual words, are all God-approved. Jesus prayed it, hence it has the highest approval. The Lord's Prayer is a gem, a gift to all men on the earth. If we can listen to the heart of Jesus, learn the elements of this prayer and implement them in our own prayer lives, our prayers would take on a new dimension. This will radically transform the way prayers are said in our homes, in our churches and our communities. Not only will our renewed prayer affect the things around us; it will radically transform our inner man through a deeper intimacy with God. As we draw nearer to God through prayer and His Word, we know more of God's heart and it makes it easier to pray according to His will.

"And this is the confidence that we have in him, that, if we ask any thing according to his will, he heareth us: And if we know that he hears us, whatsoever we ask, we know that we have the petitions that we desired of him." **I John 5:14, 15**

I do not believe that Jesus taught His disciples this prayer for no reason. God has given us these rules and principles for us to follow and obey. If a person applies for a job without reading the job description, there is a strong possibility that they will not get the job because they have ignored the requirements for the job. In the same way, the importance of prayer in the life of a Christian cannot be overemphasized. Prayer makes tremendous power available for a Christian, that is dynamic in its working. Prayer touches heaven and it changes earth. Prayer is the master key that unlocks the treasures of heaven. Prayer is the place for breaking strongholds, releasing blessings and rejoicing. Prayer is the key to a successful and fulfilling relationship with God. No wonder we need to fully understand how to pray.

This book is written out of an answer to my heart's cry, "Lord, Teach Me To Pray". I pray that as you read this book, your heart's cry will be answered too. I desire that as we look closely together at the prayer Jesus taught

His disciples, we will see the footprints, elements and principles of a healthy prayer time. As we then put these elements into our prayer time, we will be taught by God the sweet fellowship of prayer.

Happy reading and I pray this book helps to bend your knees once more.

The Lord's Prayer is quoted twice in the New Testament once in Matthew and again in Luke. This book is based on the prayer in the book of Matthew, which is the most commonly used version in the church today. I feel that it is a fuller and richer account.

Matthew's Account (Matthew 6:9-13)

> *"After this manner therefore pray ye:*
> *Our Father which art in heaven,*
> *Hallowed be thy name.*
> *Thy kingdom come,*
> *Thy will be done In earth, as it is in heaven.*
> *Give us this day our daily bread.*
> *And forgive us our debts, as we forgive our debtors.*
> *And lead us not into temptation, but deliver us from evil:*
> *For thine is the kingdom, and the power, and the glory, for ever.*
> *Amen."*

Luke's Account (Luke 11:2-4)

"And he said unto them. When ye pray, say:
Our Father which art in heaven.
Hallowed be thy name.
Thy kingdom come.
Thy will be done, as in heaven, so in earth.
Give us day by day our daily bread.
And forgive us our sins; for we also forgive every one that is indebted to us.
And lead us not into temptation; but deliver us from evil."

In this book, we will consider 21 elements to the Lord's Prayer as found in Matthew's account and these are listed below:

1. Relationship: Our Father
2. Recognition: Which art in heaven
3. Adoration: Hallowed be thy name
4. Anticipation: Thy kingdom come
5. Consecration: Thy will be done
6. Universality: In earth
7. Conformity: As it is in heaven.
8. Supplication: Give us
9. Definiteness: This day
10. Necessity: Our daily bread
11. Penitence: And forgive us
12. Obligation: Our debts
13. Forgiveness, Love, and Mercy: As we forgive our debtors
14. Guidance: And lead us
15. Protection: Not into temptation
16. Salvation: But deliver us
17. Righteousness: From evil
18. Acknowledgement and Faith: For thine is the kingdom
19. Humility and Reverence: And the power, and the glory

20. Timelessness: For ever
21. Affirmation: Amen

In the following pages, we will now examine each of these elements in turn.

The inspiration for this book came from Dake's Annotated Bible where 23 Elements of the Lord's Prayer are identified. In Dake's, forgiveness, love and mercy are separated. Here, with Dake's permission, we will consider them as one, resulting in 21 areas for examination.

Element 1
Relationship: Our Father

In the Old Testament in the bible, we read that the world was lost in sin after man handed over the authority given to him by God to the devil. The channel between God and man was blocked because of sin. God raised High Priests and a tabernacle was made for God. The Ark of the Covenant was made according to the instructions of the Lord and kept in the tabernacle. Later, the tabernacle was replaced with a static temple to house the Ark and be the place of God's presence in Israel. God dwelt among His people but man was rebellious and at times defiled the temple of the living God. God's intention from the Garden of Eden has always been to fellow¬ship with us—His creation. God wanted a relationship with man but man's sins kept making this impossible. In Isaiah, we read the prophecies concerning the coming of God's Son.

> *"For unto us a child is born, unto us a son is given: and the government shall be upon his shoulder: and his name shall be called Wonderful, Counselor, The*

mighty God, The everlasting Father, The Prince of Peace. Of the increase of [his] government and peace [there shall be] no end, upon the throne of David, and upon his kingdom, to order it, and to establish it with judgment and with justice from henceforth even for ever. The zeal of the LORD of hosts will perform this." **Isaiah 9:6,7**

To restore man's relationship with Him, God sent His Son. This was the beginning of a new relationship between God and man, a Father-Child relationship.

"For God so loved the world, that he gave his only begotten Son, that whosoever believeth in him should not perish, but have everlasting life." **John 3:16**

According to the writer of Hebrews:

"But we see Jesus, who was made a little lower than the angels for the suffering of death, crowned with glory and honour; that he by the grace of God should taste death for every man. For it became him, for whom [are] all things, and by whom [are] all things, in bringing many sons unto glory, to make the captain of their salvation perfect through sufferings" **Hebrews 2:9,10**

Jesus is the Son of God, the mighty God. He is Emmanuel,

which means, "God with us". God through Jesus came as a lamb. Hebrews 2 says He tasted of death to bring us to glory by removing the barrier of sin, through His son, so that we can become God's children and a new relationship can be formed with Our Father.

Paul, the writer of Romans, makes us understand that we were in bondage until Christ came to set us free. In chapter 8:15 he writes, "*For ye have not received the spirit of bondage again to fear; but ye have received the Spirit of adoption, whereby we cry, Abba, Father.*" He also revealed that we are lost in sin. Through John 3:16, we see that the way out of bondage is to receive the Son. We become adopted children of God by receiving His Son, As we receive Him, we can truly cry out, we can truly pray "Our Father". Through Jesus' death on the cross, our eyes are opened and we can see as God sees us. When Jesus saw Mary after his death and resurrection. He said unto her "*... but go to my brethren, and say unto them, I ascend unto my Father, and your Father; and to my God, and your God.*" John 20:17.

This is a vital portion of scripture because, for the first time in the gospels, Jesus declares that God has become our Father. Each time we pray we have an opportunity to acknowledge that we are redeemed and are God's chosen children. If God is our Father then we are heirs of His kingdom and we are joint heirs with His only begotten son, Jesus (Romans 8:17).

As you can see, the prayer starting with "Our Father" was not just for His disciples but for all who would believe in Him. We have a Father. Let us acknowledge Him each time we pray.

Element 2
Recognition: Which Art In Heaven

Does God dwell in temples made of bricks and mortar? Clearly not. Acts 17:24 says, "*God that made the world and all things therein, seeing that he is Lord of heaven and earth, dwelleth not in temples made with hands.*" God visited the temples built by the Israelites in the Old Testament but they were not His permanent residence. I was once told a story about an idol worshipper who was praying in his room one day when a madman ran into the room and knocked his idol over. When the madman left, he picked up his idol and apologized to it saying, "Sorry my god, next time I will try and protect you better". His god needed his protection. People who carry their idols in their pockets need to protect them and clean them. Our God is in heaven, our God neither slumbers nor sleeps. He is constantly watching over us. He is not dependent on us for His protection. On the contrary, He protects us! Glory to God. What a very big God we serve, even the clouds are the dust of his feet

(Nahum 1:3). It is impossible to measure or imagine how big God is.

> *"Thus saith the LORD, The heaven is my throne, and the earth is my footstool: where is the house that ye build unto me? and where [is] the place of my rest?"* **Isaiah 66:1**

God is just so awesome. We need to recognise that God rules from on high.

> *"Again he said, Therefore hear the word of the LORD; I saw the LORD sitting upon his throne, and all the host of heaven standing on his right hand and on his left."* **2 Chronicles 18:18**

> *"The LORD is in his holy temple, the LORD'S throne is in heaven: his eyes behold, his eyelids try the children of men."* **Psalms 11:4**

> *"Be not rash with thy mouth, and let not thine heart be hasty to utter any thing before God: for God is in heaven, and thou upon earth: therefore let thy words be few."* **Ecclesiastes 5:2**

We are encouraged here to watch what we say. We need to acknowledge God as Father who sees all and knows all because He created all and rules from His throne on high.

As we read in the prayer of King Solomon at the dedication of the new temple in Jerusalem, He dwells in heaven,

> *"And harken thou to the supplication of thy servant, and of thy people Israel, when they shall pray toward this place: and hear thou in heaven thy dwelling place; and when thou hearest, forgive."* **I Kings 8:30**

Although God dwells in heaven, His ears are open to our cries for help. God left His throne for our redemption and came in the form of a man. Let us learn from the Lord's example and obey God's word. Each time we pray, it is important that we recognise God's position as enthroned above the earth

Each time we pray, "Our Father which art in heaven" we are recognising God's greatness. We need to believe that our help is in heaven, hence we have no reason to trust in the arm of flesh. We trust in the God who makes His home above.

Element 3
Adoration: Hallowed Be Thy Name

Adoration is the same thing as worship. To hallow means to honour as holy, to bless, to exalt, to sanctify. Adoration is like hallowing with heartfelt affection. The Bible says that our God is a holy God. Therefore, we ought to worship Him with a right heart and attitude. We need to sanctify the Lord in our hearts.

> *"O come, let us worship and bow down: let us kneel before the LORD our maker."* **Psalms 95:6**

We are called to worship, called to come and bow our knees in worship to the Holy God who is our Father and dwells in the heavens. This is a great privi-lege. As we worship, we are declaring to the whole world and every created being that God is Holy. Not only does God live in heaven but the bible says in Revelation 4:10 that we are to worship because He lives forever. Our God is altogether amazing and His ways are wonderful. Our Father gave up His life so that we might have life. In His death is our life, and in His resurrection is our hope of eternal life.

> *"Bless the LORD, O my soul: and all that is within me, [bless] his holy name.*
> *Bless the LORD, O my soul, and forget not all his benefits:*
> *Who forgiveth all thine iniquities; who healeth all thy diseases;*
> *Who redeemeth thy life from destruction; who crowneth thee with lovingkindness and tender mercies;*
> *Who satisfieth thy mouth with good [things; so that] thy youth is renewed like the eagle's."*
> **Psalms 103: 1-5**

This portion of scripture should excite us because it reveals what God has done for us His children. He loads benefits on us. He heals us. He forgives us. He has redeemed us. He fills us with good things and crowns us with lovingkindness. What an awesome God we serve! He is worthy of praise and thanksgiving. As we bless Him and worship Him, we join with the whole host of heaven in worship and adoration of the great I Am. What should be our response to the things that the Lord has done? In the story of the ten lepers (Luke 17), only one returned to honour the giver of the gift of healing. Let us not be like the other nine who failed to adore the Most High for the things that He had done. Rather, let us follow the example of the one that fell at His feet, worshipped, and gave thanks. He honoured and adored God.

The story of the alabaster box (Luke 7:37), where the lady bows at the feet of Jesus is an example of how we can show our adoration of God. Now is the time to worship. When we pray to God we need to remember to worship Him. In John chapter four, we read Jesus' dialogue with the woman at the well in Samaria;

> *"God is a Spirit: and they that worship him must worship him in spirit and in truth. The woman saith unto him, I know that Messias cometh, which is called Christ: when he is come, he will tell us all things."* **John 4:24,25**

Jesus says that the true worshipper will worship the Father in Spirit and truth. We are called not just to be worshippers but to be true worshippers. To hallow is to hail; to hail is to worship. Each prayer must contain elements of worship because we serve a God who is worthy of our worship. Each time we worship God, we are obeying a direct command of Jesus:

> *"Then saith Jesus unto him, Get thee hence, Satan: for it is written, Thou shalt worship the Lord thy God,*

and him only shalt thou serve." **Matthew 4:10**

Our service to God reflects our heart of worship. You can only truly serve one Master; we must accept the Lordship of God and live our lives in full service to Him.

> *"For we are the circumcision, which worship God in the spirit, and rejoice in Christ Jesus, and have no confidence in the flesh."* **Philippians 3:3**

Element 4
Anticipation: Thy Kingdom Come

To anticipate something is to look forward to it. We are the children of the living God and we should always look forward to seeing God's kingdom come on this earth. God is totally good and man is totally sinful. In reality, God ought to reject man but we know that God has been merciful to mankind and has forgiven and accepted us in Christ. What is the purpose of God in our salvation? Firstly, I believe God desires our fellowship, and secondly, He desires light to shine on this earth in the midst of darkness. Man should join with Christ his Redeemer and bring to pass Christ's reign on earth.

> *"Jesus answered, My kingdom is not of this world: if my kingdom were of this world, then would my servants fight, that I should not be delivered to the Jews: but now is my kingdom not from hence."*
> **John 18:36**

Although God dwells in the heavens, we recognize that He created not just the heavens but the earth also. If God created the earth, then He has every right to rule on earth. God is counting on the church to extend His kingdom on earth by His Spirit. We are to be His witnesses on earth. This is why He put His Spirit in us (Acts 1:8). Paul reveals to us in the book of Corinthians what will happen at the end of time:

> *"Then cometh the end, when he shall have delivered up the kingdom to God, even the Father; when he shall have put down all rule and all authority and power. For he must reign, till he hath put all enemies under his feet. The last enemy that shall be destroyed is death. For he hath put all things under his feet. But when he saith all things are put under him, it is manifest that he is excepted, which did put all things under him. And when all things shall be subdued unto him, then shall the Son also himself be subject unto him that put all things under him, that God may be all in all."* **1 Corinthians 15:24-28**

As believers, we need to live in a constant state of anticipation of His return to rule. However, before this happens, we need to take more of the earth, extending God's kingdom in anticipation of His full reign. The government of the whole earth will be upon His shoulders. The last enemy, death, shall be destroyed. God is going to put all things under Christ. Even death loses its sting in the presence of Jesus. God, the Father, is totally dedicated to seeing all things under Jesus' feet. As we pray thy kingdom come we are joining with God to see the full rule of Christ. Let us, therefore, pray in sincerity, "Thy kingdom come" in our lives, in our homes, in our churches, in our offices and our communities. As we pray, we must see God taking ground with the eyes of faith. This will enable us to pray from the heart and mean it. Prayer must be from the heart. Anything from the flesh only leads to death, but the Spirit gives life. The Spirit of God lives in us to help us extend the Kingdom of God. Let us therefore continually confess our anticipation with meaning, faith, hope and joy and we will see the growth of God's kingdom.

Element 5
Consecration: Thy Will Be Done

Jesus was a practical man; He always did what He said. He led His disciples by His example. God asked Abraham to give up his son. However, before God ever asked Abraham to surrender Isaac, God had already given up His own Son. We know this because Revelation 13:8 says that Christ was slain from the foundation of the world. God was willing to give up His own Son for us. Jesus is so much like His Father. In the Lord's Prayer, Jesus teaches us to allow God to have His way in our lives. Jesus also faced this challenge. Let us look at the account in Matthew:

> *"And he went a little further, and fell on his face, and prayed, saying, O my Father, if it be possible, let this cup pass from me: nevertheless not as I will, but as thou wilt.And he cometh unto the disciples, and findeth them asleep, and saith unto Peter, What! could ye not watch with me one hour? Watch and pray, that ye enter not into temptation: the spirit indeed is*

willing, but the flesh is weak. He went away again the second time, and prayed, saying, O my Father, if this cup may not pass away from me, except I drink it, thy will be done." **Matthew 26:39-42**

In the above portion of scripture, Jesus was asking God if it was possible for the cup of suffering the death on the cross could pass over Him. As His prayer ended, He declared thy will be done. Jesus was God in the flesh and He was tempted as we are. In verse 41, Jesus addresses His disciples and (one could argue) Himself, saying: "The spirit indeed is willing, but the flesh is weak." Jesus in the flesh felt the weakness of the flesh. Through this, Jesus still wanted only one thing: that the will of God is done, so that His kingdom will come.

In 2 Timothy 1:7, the Bible tells us that God has not given us a spirit of fear. So despite the difficulties and challenges you may we faced with, your prayer should be that God's will be done. Our resolve should always be that God be glorified.

"Why art thou cast down, O my soul? and why art thou disquieted within me? hope in God: for I shall yet praise him, [who is] the health of my countenance, and my God." **Psalms 43:5**

Like David, Jesus found inner strength and He took up the challenge. He obeyed the call and allowed God to have His way. Although He was God as a man He had to submit to the will of God the Father. Jesus knew that to obey is better than sacrifice (1 Samuel 15:22).

The more we tell God "thy will he done", the more we are saying that God knows what He is doing on the earth and in our lives. We need to be in agree-ment with God and the plans He has for us. For God's will to be truly fulfilled in our lives, we must be totally submitted to His will. It takes effort on our part to be truly surrendered. As we pray, we should learn to always say: "Thy will be done, O Lord". At times in my life, I feel the pressure mounting when I have to abandon my will for His will. My mind tells me, "This is crazy", yet my spirit stirs me to obey. There are pressures all around us that will try and stop us from yielding to God's will. We just need to listen for His voice and block out the voice of the enemy, the voice of human reason, the voice of the flesh and the voice of our mind and say, "Thy will be done".

Element 6
Universality: In Earth

In the previous section, we talked about God's will being done. Here we focus on His will being done in the earth. Over the years, as I have shared my faith with different people around the world, I have been asked time and time again: If God is God, why does He allow suffering on earth? Well, God created the earth and He wanted man to have dominion over it.

> *"And God said, Let us make man in our image, after our likeness: and let them have dominion over the fish of the sea, and over the fowl of the air, and over the cattle, and over all the earth, and over every creeping thing that creepeth upon the earth."* **Genesis 1:26**

Man lost that dominion through sin but through Christ's death, we have hope of a restoration of the earth, through the church, by the working of God's spirit. The earth is still God's footstool, yet it is up to us, the church, to maintain and enforce God's rule on earth. We as believers have this unique opportunity to serve God in the flesh. It is here on earth that our service matters, for after this life is death and after that judgement.

While on earth, we must worship. On earth, God should be manifested through our lives. As Christ is the express image of God, we are called to be Christlike. Each time we pray, "Thy will be done in earth" we are pledging our earthly life to His service. If we pray "Thy will be done in earth" then our lifestyle on earth should conform to that declaration.

> *"For by him were all things created, that are in heaven, and that are in earth, visible and invisible, whether they be thrones, or dominions, or principalities, or powers: all things were created by him, and for him: And he is before all things, and by him all things consist. And he is the head of the body, the church: who is the beginning, the firstborn from the dead; that in all things he might have the preeminence."*
> **Colossians 1:16-18**

God must have pre-eminence in the earth. God has laid a claim to the earth and He is working in the earth for good. God sees all. He is in all and is working through all things in the earth for good: wars, peace, hunger, prosperity, seasons of calm and seasons of extremes. His will is going to be done in the earth.

Element 7
Conformity: As It Is In Heaven

This element, like the previous one, is linked to God's will being done. The will of God is God's clear purpose. If we are to walk with God and enjoy fellowship with Him, we must be willing to find His will for our lives and walk in it.

Conformity has to do with obedience to rules and standards. God wants us to be in agreement with Him and His will. We are not to run our lives by any other standard than the one He sets.

> *"And be not conformed to this world: but be ye transformed by the renewing of your mind, that ye may prove what is that good, and acceptable, and perfect, will of God."* **Romans 12:2**

There is a standard which God wants us to conform to as we represent Him on earth. Like ambassadors, we are a reflection of God. As we allow God's will to be done in our lives, we bring heaven to earth. In heaven, there is no opposition to the rule of God. Upon the earth, God wants to extend this same rule through man. There is coming a new heaven and a new earth; the Bible reveals this in the book of Revelation. Before the coming of the new heaven and earth, God will have total pre-eminence on this earth.

What happens in heaven? The Bible tells us that the four and twenty elders worship the Lord day and night (Revelation 19:4). We can conclude that it is the will of God for the whole of creation to worship Him. Man worshipping God delights the heart of God and the Bible says that God dwells in the praises of His people (Psalms 22:3). In heaven, the angels are ministering spirits ministering the will of God. Man should be ministering to fellow men. It delights God's heart when we dwell in unity and harmony on the earth just as the Trinity is in heaven. Jesus said, "I pray that they may be one as we are one" (John 17:11).

In heaven is holiness. God is holy and he desires that we conform to this standard of Holiness. God wants us to live as holy people.

> *"I beseech you therefore, brethren, by the mercies of God, that ye present your bodies a living sacrifice, holy, acceptable unto God, which is your reasonable*

service." Romans 12:1

Let us take the words of Paul and put them into practice so that our lives will be a manifestation of the will of God. God's will must first be done in my life as it is in heaven before I can go out and tell the whole world about it. At times, God will manifest His will through any vessel (as in the Bible stories of Balaam and the donkey, Jonah and the whale, and the earthquake and the foreign enemies of Israel). However, God's preferred method is that His heavenly will should be revealed through us. I have no doubt in my mind that if we yield to God, we will establish His rule in our generation. The key is our individual conformity to His will and our rendering of a holy service to Him and men.

Element 8
Supplication: Give Us

Here we begin to make a petition to God out of our relationship with Him. A petition is a formal request. To make a petition is to appeal, to ask and to lobby. When we have drawn near to God by acknowledging, conforming, consecrating, anticipating, and adoring, we can then begin the process of petition. Most of us start our prayers here, reading a shopping list to God without the appropriate acknowledgement of what God wants and desires. As God stirs our hearts to pray, let us remember to fully acknowledge God first before we start shopping. God is merciful and loving but he also has every right to be acknowledged. We have a good Father who loves to bless His children. Listen to the words of Christ:

> *"But when ye pray, use not vain repetitions, as the heathen do: for they think that they shall be heard for their much speaking. Be not ye therefore like unto them: for your Father knoweth what things ye have*

> *need of, before ye ask him."* **Matthew 6:7,8**

In addition, the words of King Solomon at the dedication of the temple are found in this passage of scripture.

> *"Hearken therefore unto the supplications of thy servant, and of thy people Israel, which they shall make toward this place: hear thou from thy dwelling place, [even] from heaven; and when thou hearest, forgive."* **2 Chronicles 6:21**

God is fully aware of His children's needs. The Bible says that before we ask, the Lord answers (Isaiah 65:24). Our God knows us much more than we know ourselves and if we pray according to His will, we will only get the best for our lives. He truly desires to hear and answer our requests but we must be praying His will. James 4:3 says, "*You ask and receive not because you ask amiss.*" We need to acknowledge God not just at the beginning of our prayers but through all of them. We need to submit to His will.

> *"And this is the confidence that we have in him, that, if we ask any thing according to his will, he heareth us:"* **I John 5:14**

Understanding our relationship with God is key to the rest of the Lord's Prayer because a misconception of who

God is breeds doubt. Doubt sees obstacles, doubt robs us of confidence in His presence and above all doubt fears to ask. Faith in God, on the other hand, helps us to enter God's presence with boldness in the power of His redeeming blood. The Holy Spirit is always on hand to show us how to pray as long as we abide in God. Jesus said, "If ye abide in me, and my words abide in you, ye shall ask what ye will, and it shall be done unto you." (John 15:7). The key question here is: Where are we in our relationship with God?

> *"And whatsoever we ask, we receive of him, because we keep his commandments, and do those things that are pleasing in his sight."* **I John 3:22**

Let us not hinder our approach to God with a lack of understanding of His word. Our supplication is meaningless if we do not know His word, because His word reveals His will. Prayer takes on a new dimension as we grow in our knowledge of God's word. Ignorance of God's promises is a more fatal hindrance than ignorance of our needs. John says we receive of God because we keep His commandments. What about those who do not know God's word, or are new Christians? God reveals Himself to us through His creation all around us. God draws us to Himself and He writes His laws in our hearts.

Even the people who do not believe in God listen to their conscience. God has made provision for us to pray according to His word.

Jesus said, "ask and it shall be given" (Matt 7:7). At this point in the Lord's Prayer, we are encouraged to ask for things. God knows all our needs but He still wants to hear us pray to Him. Prayer is key to developing our relationship with God. Supplication is the channel which God and man use constantly to confirm and affirm their relationship. We ask God and He answers because He hears us. If we receive answers to our requests, it encourages us to ask again. "Give us."

Finally, Jesus shows us that our supplication should be selfless. We go to God in prayer not just to ask for ourselves but also for those around us (our families, friends and foes).

ELEMENT 9
DEFINITENESS: THIS DAY

The Bible tells us that God owns time and that a year is like a day before Him. Nevertheless, He wants us to be specific about our requests to Him—specific not just in the request, but also in the timeframe. Pe¬ter said that God is not slack concerning His promises (2 Peter 3:9) and Isaiah reveals that God's ways are not like our ways (Isaiah 55:8). In Hebrews, we read:

> *"Jesus Christ the same yesterday, and to day, and for ever."* **Hebrews 13:8**

God is unchangeable. He is the same always. God is as dependable today as He will be tomorrow. We can trust in Him. Today, therefore, we can ask God to grant us our requests. In the book of Daniel, we read about Daniel's prayer on behalf of Israel. It took a while before he received his answer but the angel told him that God had answered on the same day he prayed (Daniel 9:23). God spoke to Abraham and told him that he would have a child. About 9 months before the child was born,

God visited Abraham again and said that this time the following year he would have a child. God owns time; He is the creator of time and is not bound by time, therefore let us not cast away our confidence in His ability to hear and answer.

> *"Wherefore (as the Holy Ghost saith, To day if ye will hear his voice, Harden not your hearts, as in the provocation, in the day of temptation in the wilderness...)*
> *But exhort one another daily, while it is called To day; lest any of you be hardened through the de¬ceitfulness of sin."* **Hebrews 3:7,8,13**

Apart from touching on time, this element also touches on our faith. Do we have faith in the ability of God to answer prayer? If we do, then we need to ask in the light of God's ability and not be limited by our thoughts of what we think God can do.

Let us arise as men and women of faith, exercising our faith and asking God, "Give us this day" out of our relationship with Him. If we hold fast the confession of our faith, we will see answers to prayers today, not tomorrow. The writer of Hebrews encourages us to exhort each other daily (while it is called today). Today is the day of salvation; today is the day of res¬toration. God wants to manifest Himself in our daily lives. Knowing the God we serve enables us to have:

1. A full assurance of faith
2. Confidence
3. A solid conviction
4. An unwavering heart that is based on God's word.

These four things are all characteristics of faith. Faith in God enables us to be definite in our requests to God, knowing that it is done. Amen.

ELEMENT 10
NECESSITY: OUR DAILY BREAD

Our daily bread speaks of our necessary or essential needs. To understand this element in context, let us look at elements 8,9 and 10 together. "Give us this day our daily bread." Here is a definite supplication for a daily necessity. It is a supplication in faith for a need that is important (our daily bread), which will sustain us throughout the day, not just physically but also spiritually.

The basis of this prayer is that God knows what we need. These are the words of Jesus:

> *"If ye then, being evil, know how to give good gifts unto your children, how much more shall your Father which is in heaven give good things to them that ask him?"* **Matthew 7:11**

> *"Be not ye therefore like unto them: for your Father knoweth what things ye have need of, before ye ask him."* **Matthew 6:8**

Fundamentally, God cares about us. He is our refuge,

our helper and our strong tower so says the Psalmist. Therefore, we can lean on the Lord for our every need. Paul had a revelation of this and wrote in his letter to the Philippians:

> *"But my God shall supply all your need according to his riches in glory by Christ Jesus."* **Philippians 4:19**

The scriptures reveal that all our needs shall be met. God knows what things we need and He will meet those needs in our lives. King Asa declares in 2 Chronicles 14:11 that God can help both the mighty and the powerless. It does not matter what your status is. In Christ, your needs are met according to God's promise. We need to understand that ultimately God Himself provides our daily bread. Our daily bread does not come from our jobs, our investments, or our friends – it is God that provides for us through those means. God desires that we work with our hands on the earth, but He is the one that provides bread for the eater and seed for the sower (2 Corinthians 9:10). We need to know that when we are in God we shall not lack physically, spiritually or mentally. Therefore, we need to learn the art of not worrying, for God is the provider of our daily bread.

> *"Two things have I required of thee; deny me them not before I die: Remove far from me vanity and lies:*

give me neither poverty nor riches; feed me with food convenient for me: Lest I be full, and deny thee, and say. Who is the LORD? Or lest I be poor, and steal, and take the name of my God in vain."
Proverbs 30:7-9

The above portion of scripture is a very good guide to what our needs are. A lot of people would look at this scripture and think our needs include our cravings, the stuff we lust after, our wants or wishes. No! This scripture is dealing with our needs. The Father who provides your needs know what you need and will meet that need. This is the promise we must believe in faith. James talked about asking amiss and fulfilling our lust as being one reason why we do not receive answers to our prayers (James 4:3).

Each time we pray, "Give us this day our daily bread," let us expect our needs to be met and not our wants. As our needs are met, let us continue to be a blessing to others, meeting their needs as God enables us to.

Element 11
Penitence: And Forgive Us

As a modern-day believer, I would have started my prayer here, asking for forgiveness before asking for my daily bread. Jesus did not. He started His prayer based on relationship. This has been a revelation to me. God knows us, yet He has compassion on us and hears us. Why did Jesus pray this prayer? He was without sin, yet on our behalf, He showed penitence for sin in His prayer. No wonder He could bear the sins of the world.

Jesus is showing us a pattern, revealing both the ability of God to pardon and His love for a contrite heart. We need revealed knowledge in this area. Let us look at a few scriptures:

> *"Look upon mine affliction and my pain; and forgive all my sins."* **Psalms 25:18**

> *"Take with you words, and turn to the LORD: say unto him, Take away all iniquity, and receive us graciously: so will we render the calves of our lips."* **Hosea 14:2**

"If we confess our sins, he is faithful and just to forgive us our sins, and to cleanse us from all unrighteousness."
I John 1:9

The key to forgiveness here is to request it from a loving Father. We must confess our sins to God and He is willing and able to forgive us. There is no point trying to hide our sins from God and in fact, the Bible encourages us to confess our sins to each other. God sees all and He knows all. He just requires us to be humble enough to approach Him. Jesus, by His death, has opened the veil that separated us from God. Now that the veil is torn, we can approach God with boldness to obtain mercy (Hebrew 4:16). We can approach God and we can receive His love and mercy.

Our God is holy and hates iniquity. God rebukes workers of iniquity (Matthew 23:28), and He rejects workers of iniquity (Luke 13:27). We are encouraged not to rejoice in iniquity (1 Corinthians 13:6). Paul encourages Timothy that people who call on God must depart from iniquity (2 Tim 2:19).

Each time we pray, "Forgive us", we should also make a commitment in our hearts to depart from iniquity. If we do sin, let us just cry out to God, "Forgive us". Once we have His forgiveness, we should be grateful to Him.

Element 12
Obligation: Our Debts

To obligate is to bind to do something or agree to do something. We are compelled by the requirements of an obligation to uphold our end of the bargain. It is similar to a contract, where we agree to do something and where failure on our part makes us indebted to another. By virtue of our new birth in Christ, we are obligated to obey God. The whole world is under that obligation but we as believers, are much more so. When we sin, we are breaking our obligation and we are indebted to God. If we combine elements 11 (Penitence) and 12 together, we get, "forgive us our debts" (sins, shortcomings, trespasses, failures, and bad conduct).

How come we sin? The simple answer is that it is in our nature. When Adam sinned, the entire human race became partakers of sin. In Christ alone is this sinful nature changed and transformed. Yet, after Christ comes into our lives, we still seem to battle with sin. To win the battle, we need to renew our minds and yield to the spirit of God. For as many as are led by the Spirit of God are the Sons of God. (Romans 8:14). We need more than just our daily bread from God; we also need deliverance from the works of the flesh. God can forgive. He can impute righteousness and remove our guilt and our sin.

> *"Owe no man any thing, but to love one another: for he that loveth another hath fulfilled the law."*
> **Romans 13:8**

A prayer:

Lord, if we fail to love, we fail you and we become debtors. Forgive us our debts and pour your heart into our life.

Element 13
Forgiveness, Love, and Mercy: As We Forgive Our Debtors

The amazing thing about this element is that elements 11 (Penitence) and 12 (Obligation) get us into God's presence, yet that entrance is conditional as revealed here. The pattern is this: God forgives us as we forgive others. The key to being forgiven by God is forgiving others. To get a fuller understanding of this element, let us read a parable of Jesus:

'Then came Peter to him, and said, Lord, how oft shall my brother sin against me, and I forgive him? till seven times? Jesus saith unto him, I say not unto thee, Until seven times: but, Until seventy times seven.

Therefore is the kingdom of heaven likened unto a certain king, which would take account of his servants. And when he had begun to reckon, one was brought unto him, which owed him ten thousand talents.

But forasmuch as he had not to pay, his lord commanded

him to be sold, and his wife, and children, and all that he had, and payment to be made. The servant therefore fell down, and worshipped him, saying. Lord, have patience with me, and I will pay thee all.

Then the lord of that servant was moved with compassion, and loosed him, and forgave him the debt. But the same servant went out, and found one of his fellowservants, which owed him an hundred pence; and he laid hands on him, and took him by the throat, saying. Pay me that thou owest.

And his fellowservant fell down at his feet, and besought him, saying. Have patience with me, and I will pay thee all. And he would not: but went and cast him into prison, till he should pay the debt. So when his fellowservants saw what was done, they were very sorry, and came and told unto their lord all that was done.

Then his lord, after that he had called him, said unto him, O thou wicked servant, I forgave thee all that debt, because thou desiredst me: Shouldest not thou also have had compassion on thy fellowservant, even as I had pity on thee? And his lord was wroth, and delivered him to the tormentors, till he should pay all that was due unto him.

So likewise shall my heavenly Father do also unto you, if ye from your hearts forgive not every one his brother their trespasses." **Matthew 18:21-35**

This passage reveals very clearly how forgiveness ought to operate in our lives. It reveals that we must forgive as we have been forgiven. In verses 26 and 27, we see that the Lord had compassion and He forgave. Compassion means to be considerate, to be kind and caring. Compassion is like love mixed with mercy. Jesus was compassionate and this led to His death on the cross. His death brought forgiveness to us. The man in verse 26 asked for forgiveness and the king had mercy on him and showed him love by forgiving him. In verse 28, we see a very unfortunate turn of events when the forgiven man approached one who owed him money. He took his debtor by the throat and demanded his money. Then, just as he had done, his fellowservant asks for pardon but he refused and threw him in prison.

These events proved that the servant was a wicked man. The people around him could not hold their peace any longer and they reported it to the king. Let us step back to verses 21 and 22 where Jesus reveals to His disciples and to us too, the challenge of constantly forgiving those who sin against us. God has made a way for our forgiveness in

Christ and we as God's children must be like our forgiving Father. Love is a powerful force. Love is kind, love thinks no evil, bears all things, believes all things, and endures all things (1 Corinthians 13:2-7). Love is the tool that makes forgiveness a reality. Without love, it is difficult to forgive. Mercy proceeds from love. And forgiveness is proof of love in our hearts and our lives.

We are to constantly forgive those who sin against us, 70x7 that is 490 times as Jesus said this is what is required of us. Wow! I believe it will be easier to keep forgiving others than to try and keep track of how often people have sinned against us. At our new birth in Christ, God does not only forgive us. He purges our sins (Hebrew 1:3). When God forgives, He also forgets our sins. The counter is reset each time on our behalf. "For I will be merciful to their unrighteousness, and their sins and their iniquities will I remember no more." (Heb 8:12). People might look at this and say we have a license to sin. No, we don't. Rather, we have the key to being a forgiver and shower of mercy. If I have been forgiven, then I should be more willing to forgive.

The servant in the passage of scripture was not willing to forgive so the king revoked his forgiveness. This leads me to the next point: when you combine elements 11

(Penitence), 12 (Obligation) and 13 (Forgiveness, love and mercy), it becomes obvious that our forgiveness is conditional just as the ser-vant's forgiveness was conditional. He broke the terms of the agreement by being unforgiving to his fellowservant. Our King's expectation of us is that we forgive others as He has forgiven us. During the process of our salvation, God by His Spirit reveals our sinful nature to us and then He forgives us. At the cross, God put the sins of the world (past, present and future) on Christ and forgave all sins. All we have to do is accept that forgiveness and give the same level of forgiveness to others. Some might say, "What if they do not repent?" Then we must be like Jesus, who forgave us even before we came to Him in repentance. If we are willing to forgive others, we set a seal on our forgiveness in Christ.

If we don't forgive people who sin against us, we are judging ourselves and God cannot forgive us even though a provision has been made for us to be forgiven. Our God is faithful. All He requires from us is to forgive and we will be forgiven. God is not mocked. I must expect to reap what I sow. If I sow forgiveness, then I reap forgiveness in Christ. Forgive us our debts, as we forgive our debtors.

A Prayer:

Father, Lord of heaven and earth, thank you for sending Jesus to die on the cross for me. Thank you for making such a sacrifice for my life. Lord, help me in my daily life to forgive those who sin against me. Lord, enable me by your Spirit to be forgiving. In Jesus' Name.

Element 14
Guidance: And Lead Us

To give guidance is to lead, give direction, regulate, and manage. When you travel to a foreign country and you want to go exploring, you are encouraged to go with a tour guide mainly because they have travelled those paths before and can help you on your journey. Jesus said, "I am the way, the truth and the life." Not only is He a good guide but the road we travel is His too.

> *"He maketh me to lie down in green pastures: he leadeth nne beside the still waters."* **Psalms 23:2**

The Lord is our shepherd and we know that the shepherd leads the sheep to green pastures. There is an important reality here that comes from the words "lead us". When we say "lead us" we are saying to the Lord that we do not know the way. We are acknowledging the fact that we need to trust God for direction. The great encouragement that we have as we look to God for direction is that Jesus is the way, the truth and the life.

As we say "lead us", we are not only seeking physical guidance but spiritual guidance also. God's Spirit leads us into all truth. God, by His Spirit, leads us. We get our direction and guidance from Him for all dimensions of life. Jesus, in praying this prayer is clear about the Father's will to lead us.

Each time we say "lead us", we are surrendering our whole self (spirit, soul and body) to God. To be led by God, we must leave behind every element of self. There is a tendency to say "lead us" and then still peek at our route planner, our compass, or our map and try to make our way. Jesus' assurance to us is that He is the way. Therefore, let us be wholly committed to following Him. To be truly led, you must follow. Listen to the Psalmist:

> *"For thou art my rock and my fortress; therefore for thy name's sake lead me, and guide me."*
> **Psalms 31:3**

God is willing to guide us continually.

> *"And the LORD shall guide thee continually, and satisfy thy soul in drought, and make fat thy bones: and thou shalt be like a watered garden, and like a spring of water, whose waters fail not."* **Isaiah 58:11**

As we allow God to lead us, we walk in a new dimension

of life—a dimension where we have to yield to God's direction, where we live totally under God's instructions. We must be totally committed to yield to the voice of our shepherd.

> *"For I know the thoughts that I think toward you, saith the LORD, thoughts of peace, and not of evil, to give you an expected end."* **Jeremiah 29:11**

Element 15
Protection: Not Into Temptation

To protect is to keep safe, to shield, to secure or to defend. It has a strong connection with guidance. Combining the two elements, we have "lead us not into temptation". The gravity of this prayer is so amazing that if we fully believe it as we pray it from our hearts, we will live a life that is pleasing to God.

The walls of a city are the shield of that city. The moment the walls fall or are destroyed or burnt down, that city is in trouble. The account of the walls of Jericho in the Bible confirms this. In the book of Nehemiah, Nehemiah first rebuilt the walls of Jerusalem. He knew the importance of having defences in place. This element is a cry to God, "protect us".

Psalm 144 verse 2 declares that God is our deliverer and He is our shield. A shield to a soldier is like a wall for a city. The shield of faith spoken of in Ephesians is a tool of defence. The wall acts as a defender and protector of all that lies within it.

The following portions of scripture describe the Lord as our shield:

> *"The LORD [is] my strength and my shield; my heart trusted in him, and I am helped: therefore my heart greatly rejoiceth; and with my song will I praise him."* **Psalms 28:7**

> *"But thou, O LORD, [art] a shield for me; my glory, and the lifter up of mine head."* **Psalms 3:3**

> *"Behold, O God our shield, and look upon the face of thine anointed."* **Psalms 84:9**

Several more scriptures reveal God as our defender. In connecting guidance in the previous element to protection in this, we have "lead us not into temptation" or, "steer us away from the opportunity to sin."

To tempt is either to test or try something or someone. All through scripture, God "proves" His children.

> *"And he cried unto the LORD; and the LORD shewed him a tree, [which] when he had cast into the waters, the waters were made sweet: there he made for them a statute and an ordinance, and there he proved them,"* **Exodus 15:25**

Proving is very different from tempting. To prove is to ascertain, or to confirm or establish. God proves us His children and He has every right to do this. However, He does not tempt us with evil.

> *"Blessed is the man that endureth temptation: for when he is tried, he shall receive the crown of life, which the Lord hath promised to them that love him. Let no man say when he is tempted, I am tempted of God: for God cannot be tempted with evil, neither tempteth he any man: But every man is tempted, when he is drawn away of his own lust, and enticed. Then when lust hath conceived, it bringeth forth sin: and sin, when it is finished, bringeth forth death."*
> **James 1:12-15**

In light of what James says in verse 14, we can rephrase "lead us not into temptation" to "protect us from our own lusts". Sin is a result of yielding to temptation. Sin results in death, this is how serious sin is. We need God's help; we need God's protection from ourselves. If we give in to the lust in our hearts, we will yield to temptation. We need to be led by God in our daily lives so that when temptation comes, we can always see the way of escape.

> *"There hath no temptation taken you but such as is common to man: but God is faithful, who will not*

suffer you to be tempted above that ye are able; but will with the temptation also make a way to escape, that ye may be able to bear it." **1 Corinthians 10:13**

If we allow the Holy Spirit to be our guide, then we are sure to see the way of escape from any temptation. Similarly, if we do not yield to the Spirit, God cannot be our shield and defender and we will fall into temptation. According to the book of James, we should rejoice in temptation because not yielding to it builds faith and patience.

In my walk with God, I have learnt that the fact that there is a way of escape, does not mean that I would automatically choose it. It takes a conscious effort to follow God out of the traps of temptation. As I look back on my life, I see blunders that could have been easily avoided if I had totally trusted God and taken the way of escape. As we go through life, let us be aware and be ready to take the ways of escape provided to us. This is key to us not sinning.

Each time we pray "lead us not into temptation", let us close our ears to the voice of the evil tempter, the devil. Jesus was tempted in every way, yet without sin. Jesus knew how to use the word of God as a way of escape. Let us learn from Jesus. The disciples received great wisdom from Jesus on the night of His betrayal:

> *"Watch and pray, that ye enter not into temptation: the spirit indeed is willing, but the flesh is weak."*
> **Matthew 26:41**

Those who have ears, let them hear, let them act and they will escape.

Element 16
Salvation: But Deliver Us

Salvation can also be called deliverance. In Christ, we have a Saviour and we have a deliverer. When the children of Israel were in bondage in Egypt, they cried out for a deliverer. God heard their cry and sent Moses to deliver them. God delivered them with many signs and wonders. Pharaoh resisted, but eventually (after much mourning and crying amongst the Egyptians), Pharaoh let the Isrealites go. By the leading and direction of God, Moses was their deliverer. In Exodus 14, something incredible happened. Having let the people go, Pharaoh changed his mind and pursued them to bring them back. The people of Israel panicked.

> *"And they said unto Moses, Because [there were] no graves in Egypt, hast thou taken us away to die in the wilderness? wherefore hast thou dealt thus with us, to carry us forth out of Egypt?"* **Exodus 14:11**

We see here that the people were looking up to Moses. Thank God that Moses knew he had no power of his own and that he was just the middleman. Moses knew that the signs and wonders were the work of God's power, hence he presented the Lord to the people as the only source of deliverance:

> *"And Moses said unto the people. Fear ye not, stand still, and see the salvation of the LORD, which he will shew to you to day: for the Egyptians whom ye have seen to day, ye shall see them again no more for ever. The LORD shall fight for you, and ye shall hold your peace."* **Exodus 14:13,14**

Moses was speaking prophetically into the situation. As we read on, God instructed Moses to stretch out his rod over the Red Sea. The sea opened up and the people crossed on dry ground. This was God at work bringing deliverance by the hand of Moses. Once they crossed over, they saw the waters swallow up Pharaoh and his army. They could then continue their journey in peace because God completely delivered them.

John the Baptist was a prophet in Jesus' time. He preached forgiveness of sins and the baptism of repentance which leads to salvation. At that time, salvation was linked primarily to deliverance from a sinful life. John also preached about the wrath of God which was to come. He preached that the nation needed a deliverer, not on a national level, but on an individual level. We all need to escape the consequence of sin and the only way to obtain deliverance is through God's son, Jesus.

The Psalmist had a clear revelation of God as a deliverer:

> *"The LORD is my rock, and my fortress, and my deliverer; my God, my strength, in whom I will trust; my buckler, and the horn of my salvation, and my high tower."* **Psalms 18:2**

> *"But I am poor and needy; yet the Lord thinketh upon me: thou [art] my help and my deliverer; make no tarrying, O my God."* **Psalms 40:17**

> *"Help us, O God of our salvation, for the glory of thy name: and deliver us, and purge away our sins, for thy name's sake."* **Psalms 79:9**

> *"My goodness, and my fortress; my high tower, and my deliverer; my shield, and he in whom I trust; who subdueth my people under me."* **Psalms 144:2**

The three Hebrew boys in the book of Daniel trusted God for deliverance from the fiery furnace. They were in this situation because they refused to worship idols. As a result of their disobedience to the king, they were sent to die in the fire. Below is their last statement before they were thrown into the fire:

> *"If it be so, our God whom we serve is able to deliver us from the burning fiery furnace, and he will deliver us out of thine hand, O king. But if not, be it known unto thee, O king, that we will not serve thy gods, nor worship the golden image which thou hast set up."*
> **Daniel 3:17,18**

From this statement, you can see that they had total confidence in their God's ability to deliver and they were willing to trust Him. As believers who trust in Jesus, we should trust in God's ability to deliver, not only from sin, but also from all possible dangers, trials, and temptations. Father, lead us not into temptation but constantly deliver us.

Element 17
Righteousness: From Evil

Every human being tries once in a while to do good works. God judges our good works, not by the outcome but by the underlying motives and intentions and we can only truly do good works with God's help. Isaiah makes this clear:

> *"But we are all as an unclean thing, and all our righteousness are as filthy rags; and we all do fade as a leaf; and our iniquities, like the wind, have taken us away."* **Isaiah 64:6**

Sin and unrighteousness have been passed down to all generations from the Garden of Eden. We have all sinned, thus our righteous acts are but filthy rags.

"Why are our good works seen as evil?" you may ask. The truth is that we need God's deliverance from our sinful nature. Sin can be defined as wrong-doing or disobedience. Sin robs man-made righteous¬ness of power and leaves in its place dirt and filth. It is our unrighteousness that separates us from God.

As a child, I lost a lot of treats and praise because of my constant wrongdoing. I remember on one occa¬sion I helped my mum collect her delivery of Coca-Cola from the delivery van. In the process though, I dropped a crate breaking all 24 bottles. When my mother returned, she was pleased with the work I had done but sad at her financial loss. My good work was nullified by the broken crate; I needed a deliv¬erer. A neighbour paid for the broken crate and my good deed could now be celebrated.

Likewise, if we want to be celebrated, we need to be delivered from the sinful nature we have within us as human beings. It is only in God that true good works are done. Don't get me wrong, there are lots of people all over the world trying to be good neighbours. The problem is that the God of the universe requires clean hands to deliver good works. On our own, without God, all our righteous deeds are just like filthy rags. The challenge for believers, who trust God's ability to deliver, is for us to go into the world and do the works of God as Jesus did.

> *"How God anointed Jesus of Nazareth with the Holy Ghost and with power: who went about do¬ing good, and healing all that were oppressed of the devil; for God was with him,"* **Acts 10:38**

Once we see our need for a saviour and we accept Jesus as our Saviour, He deposits righteousness in our lives and then we can truly do good works.

Jesus had to die so that we could truly live. He was righteous, which means that He had a right standing with God. He became sin for us that we might be-come the righteousness of God.

> *"For he hath made him to be sin for us, who knew no sin; that we might be made the righteousness of God in him."* **2 Corinthians 5:21**

> *"For if by one man's offence death reigned by one; much more they which receive abundance of grace and of the gift of righteousness shall reign in life by one, Jesus Christ."* **Romans 5:17**

> *"Yea doubtless, and I count all things but loss for the excellency of the knowledge of Christ Jesus my Lord: for whom I have suffered the loss of all things, and do count them but dung, that I may win Christ, And be found in him, not having mine own right¬eousness, which is of the law, but that which is through the faith of Christ, the righteousness which is of God by faith:"* **Philippians 3:8,9**

One result of deliverance from evil is the impartation of God's righteousness on us. This righteousness is received by faith in the finished work on the cross. The Lord is the source of our righteousness. Jeremiah declares "... the Lord our Righteousness" (Jeremiah 23:6). Sin is conquered by the righteousness of God.

> *"Blessed are they which do hunger and thirst after righteousness: for they shall be filled."*
> **Matthew 5:6**

A Prayer:
Deliver us from evil – Lord, thank You for sending a Saviour who delivers us from evil and imparts His righteousness into our lives.

Element 18
Acknowledgement and Faith: For Thine Is The Kingdom

God is the maker of the heavens and the earth. He is our God. David understood God; indeed God called him "a man after my heart". David loved to bless God, he loved to worship Him, and he loved to adore God. Wherever possible, he acknowledged God for who God is.

> *"Wherefore David blessed the LORD before all the congregation: and David said, Blessed be thou, LORD God of Israel our father, for ever and ever. Thine, O LORD, is the greatness, and the power, and the glory, and the victory, and the majesty: for all that is in the heaven and in the earth is thine; thine is the kingdom, O LORD, and thou art exalted as head above all."* **1 Chronicles 29:10,11**

Hear the declaration of the seventh Angel;

> *"And the seventh angel sounded; and there were great*

voices in heaven, saying. The kingdoms of this world are become the kingdoms of our Lord, and of his Christ; and he shall reign for ever and ever."
Revelation 11:15

"Thine is the kingdom" – This is a powerful statement. Element 4 (Anticipation) anticipates the coming of God's kingdom but at this point (having been forgiven, having our needs met, having received guidance, protection, righteousness and salvation), we find ourselves back at a place where we are called to acknowledge God. This further confirms to my heart that the Lord's Prayer is a pattern. For some of us, it is easy to step through all the elements. For others, it takes a while. At times, we get delayed at element 12 (Obligation) as we have to fulfil our obligations before we can move on. The key to this element is to see God, not through our own eyes, but through the eyes of Jesus. Jesus knew that God owns the king¬doms of heaven and the kingdoms of earth. Paul makes us understand that the subduing of the kingdoms will be done by Jesus:

"Then cometh the end, when he shall have deliv¬ered up the kingdom to God, even the Father; when he shall have put down all rule and all au¬thority and power. For he must reign, till he hath put all enemies

under his feet." **2 Corinthians 15:24,25**

As Jesus taught us this prayer. He could see all things subdued and He acknowledged that God the Father owns the kingdoms. Every knee would bow in acknowledgement of God's reign.

> *"For by him were all things created, that are in heaven, and that are in earth, visible and invisible, whether they be thrones, or dominions, or princi¬palities, or powers: all things were created by him, and for him: And he is before all things, and by him all things consist."* **Colossians 1:16,17**

Here we see Jesus, God the Son, as the creator of all things. We need to live the rest of our days in faith, knowing that this whole creation belongs to God. As we acknowledge His rule on the earth, our faith will be strengthened. Faith comes by hearing. The kingdoms of this world are become the king¬doms of our Lord and Christ.

Element 19
Humility and Reverence: And The Power, And The Glory

The book of Proverbs reveals that the fear of God is the beginning of wisdom (Proverbs 1:7). God is to be feared in the earth, firstly because He owns all the kingdoms of the earth. God rules with power and glory. We could rephrase this element, "Thine is the power, thine is the glory". As we look upon the sacrifice He made for us to be redeemed and the humility of His death on the cross, we could lose sight of Jesus' awesome power and ultimate victory over death.

At this point in the prayer, Jesus refocuses our attention on God. The prayer starts with God and ends with God.

God delivered Israel with great power:

> *"And Moses besought the LORD his God, and said, LORD, why doth thy wrath wax hot against thy people, which thou hast brought forth out of the land of Egypt with great power, and with a mighty hand?"*
> **Exodus 32:11**

Ezra knew the power of God:

"For I was ashamed to require of the king a band of soldiers and horsemen to help us against the enemy in the way: because we had spoken unto the king, saying. The hand of our God is upon all them for good that seek him; but his power and his wrath is against all them that forsake him." **Ezra 8:22**

The Psalmist was convinced that God has power:

"God hath spoken once; twice have I heard this; that power belongeth unto God." **Psalms 62:11**

These scriptures should inspire reverence from us, God's people. We should be grateful to God for His awesome power, His saving power, His healing power, His creative power and the power of His love for us.

"And ye said, Behold, the LORD our God hath shewed us his glory and his greatness, and we have heard his voice out of the midst of the fire: we have seen this day that God doth talk with man, and he liveth." **Deuteronomy 5:24**

"The heavens declare the glory of God; and the firmament sheweth his handywork." **Psalms 19:1**

"Declare his glory among the heathen, his wonders among all people." **Psalms 96:3**

"The LORD is high above all nations, and his glory above the heavens." **Psalms 113:4**

"Thou art worthy, O Lord, to receive glory and honour and power: for thou hast created all things, and for thy pleasure they are and were created." **Revelation 4:11**

The reality is that our God is awesome in power and glory. When we look at all He went through to deliver us, we should never forget His awesome power. God is worthy to receive our praise. We should adore Him. He seeks reverent and humble worshippers. God is awesome in splendour and even the heavens declare His glory.

"The heavens declare his righteousness, and all the people see his glory." **Psalms 97:6**

As God's children, let us continue to revere Him for His saving power, His creative power, His sustaining power, His healing power and the power of His love. Let us join the angels and say;

"Glory to God in the highest, and on earth peace, good will toward men." **Luke 2:14**

We just need to ascribe greatness to our God, for He is the rock of our salvation. His works are perfect and all His ways are just. He is a faithful God, mighty in power.

> *"For the earth shall be filled with the knowledge of the glory of the LORD, as the waters cover the sea."*
> **Habakkuk 2:14**

Element 20
Timelessness: For Ever

The God we serve is not bound by time. God has control over time.

> *"But, beloved, be not ignorant of this one thing, that one day is with the Lord as a thousand years, and a thousand years as one day."* **2 Peter 3:8**

To our God, time is boundless. God lives in eter¬nity, a timeless age. Before the foundation of the earth, there was God. Genesis 1:1 can be read as: "In the eter¬nal past..." Jesus, God the Son is revealed as the Al¬pha and the Omega, the beginning and the end. God is alive forever, has been alive forever and will live forever.

Having a God that can move throughout time should be an encouragement to us. Our God is the Ancient of Days (Daniel 7:13). This same God chose us and saved us before the foundations of the world.

> *"According as he hath chosen us in him before the foundation of the world, that we should be holy and without blame before him in love:"* **Ephesians 1:4**

Element 21
Affirmation: Amen

Amen means "so be it". To affirm is to state a fact or to declare as true. Amen is said after a prayer as a seal, a lid, or as a conclusion to all that has been spoken. The Lord our God is the true God, Amen.

> *"And unto the angel of the church of the Laodiceans write; These things saith the Amen, the faithful and true witness, the beginning of the creation of God"* **Revelation 3:14**

The Scriptures end with the word, Amen. A seal on the entire written word of God.

> *"The grace of our Lord Jesus Christ be with you all. Amen."* **Revelation 22:21**

The Lord's Prayer ends with "Amen" as an affirmation of all that has been prayed.

I trust that God has revealed His person to you through the words of this book. Amen.

Let us read the Lord's Prayer with Understanding from Matthew's Account:

"After this manner therefore pray ye:

Our Father which art in heaven,

Hallowed be thy name.

Thy kingdom come,

Thy will be done In earth, as it is in heaven.

Give us this day our daily bread.

And forgive us our debts, as we forgive our debtors.

And lead us not into temptation, but deliver us from evil:

For thine is the kingdom, and the power, and the glory, for ever.

Amen."

Matthew 6:9-13

Also by Olusola Osinoiki

The Robe & The Blanket

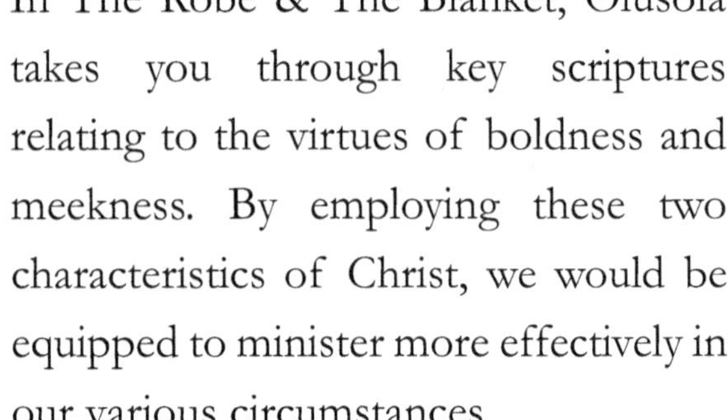

In The Robe & The Blanket, Olusola takes you through key scriptures relating to the virtues of boldness and meekness. By employing these two characteristics of Christ, we would be equipped to minister more effectively in our various circumstances

Managing Up for Career Progression

This book looks back over my journey and serves as a navigation guide to help people manage their managers in various work environments. The strategies shared in this book will equip readers with tools that will enable them navigate their real-life situations and achieve career progression.

Highway of Holiness

This book examines the subject of holiness and reveals several keys that we can follow in our pursuit of holiness. Through practical application of Scripture, Sola demonstrates what the fruit of a holy life will look like and explores how we can hope to maintain a godly lifestyle.

Four Things God Requires of Us

This book explores what God requires of us along with the benefits of obeying Him.

www.ingramcontent.com/pod-product-compliance
Lightning Source LLC
LaVergne TN
LVHW010630100826
845148LV00014B/3179
9781737590590